Anonymous

An Appeal from the Hasty to the deliberative Judgment

of the People of England

Anonymous

An Appeal from the Hasty to the deliberative Judgment
of the People of England

ISBN/EAN: 9783337059163

Printed in Europe, USA, Canada, Australia, Japan

Cover: Foto ©ninafisch / pixelio.de

More available books at **www.hansebooks.com**

A N

A P P E A L

FROM THE

H A S T Y

TO THE

DELIBERATIVE JUDGMENT

OF THE

PEOPLE OF ENGLAND,

CONTAINING

A Statement of the manifold Services rendered by our Fellow-countrymen in India, and the undeniable Claim they
poffefs to the Applaufe of their Country,—to their good
Fellowfhip and Efteem.

ALSO,

Vindicating the Characters of the MANY from the Imputations
thrown on them by the Conduct of a FEW.

TOGETHER WITH

Some important Hints to Minifters, and to the Nation in
General ; but more *immediately* valuable to the Shipping
Interefts of this Kingdom ; and humbly recommended to
the Perufal of the Members of an auguft Affembly, during the Difcuffion of the Bengal Petition now before them.

L O N D O N:

Printed for J. DEBRETT, oppofite Burlington-Houfe,
in Piccadilly.

M DCC LXXXVII,

To the P U B L I C.

INDIA DELINQUENCY having become ſo much a general topic, and ſo much is it the rage, indiſcriminately to include in the obloquy every ſubjeét of this kingdom employed in India, that natural juſtice to ſo large and reſpeétable a body of my countrymen, who labour under the unprovoked injury of ſo univerſal and unfounded a prejudice, has induced me to offer the following thoughts to the Public, on a ſubjeét, which, though not perſonally concerned in, I have conſidéred with that cool and impartial deliberation, which, the paſſions of prejudiced people, ſoured by the conduét of a guilty FEW, have rendered them incapable of exercifing for the innocent MANY. My intention is not to ſcreen the guilty, but to reſcue the innocent from

A 2

illiberal

illiberal opprobrium. The juſtice and candour of my countrymen is ſuch, that in this I can have little more to do than to place before them, in a conſpicuous and conciſe point of view, the relative ſituation which our countrymen in India bear to us, and which the hurry of reſentments only can have occaſioned ſo liberal minded a People to loſe ſight of,

TRUTH.

A N

A P P E A L,

&c.

IT is not, at any time, either an eafy or a plea-
fant tafk to contend againft prejudices; but
becomes a ftill more difficult and difcouraging
labour, when thofe prejudices, however ill-founded originally, have taken root with time, and
been fuffered to grow into conftructive facts and
admitted data, for want of fimple contradiction.
Such is the frailty or degeneracy of human nature, that the mind of man is infinitely more
prone to cenfure and condemn, even unarraigned
and unheard, than to admit merit where due,
or, where merit cannot be denied, to beftow en-
comium

comium however deferved, however confpicu-
oufly juft; and this it's depraved appetite is ever
voracioufly ready to feize any object, any pre-
tence, or even rumour, however fictitious or
problematical, that can countenance or gratify
it's rage, or juftify it's unprovoked rancour. We
cannot but reflect with aftonifhment, and our
fenfes muft revolt at the idea, that, amongft
men of the moft enlightened underftanding,
whofe minds have been cultivated and embellifh-
ed by every liberal adornment within the fpheres
of the firft feminaries of education and learn-
ing in the known world, fuch difpofitions, fo
diametrically oppofite, fo difgraceful, fo libellous
to that wonderful work of nature, Man, fhould
exift; but, painful as the idea is, the fact is in-
controvertible, and the hiftory of the prefent, as
well as paft time, comprifes but too true and
ftriking a likenefs of this portrait of deformity.---
If we turn our thoughts and reflections to the
Weftern World, and contemplate at all the fcene
which, for a feries of time, there employed the
ableft and wifeft counfels of the People of England, and the dreadful iffue and confequences of
it, we fhall find, that it *originated in prejudice,*

was *conducted in ignorance,* and has *concluded in
rivetted obstinacy, anger, and compulsive severance:*
---that we lost thirteen rich and beautiful provinces, and as many millions of good, faithful, brave,
and loyal subjects,---and all, becaufe we were
moft *unnaturally prejudiced* againft our fellow-
fubjects, whofe coats we unfeelingly endeavoured
to tear from their backs:---becaufe we were ignorant of their ftrength, miftruftful of their fidelity, difdainful of their judgment; and, fcornfully
rejecting that quantum of aid which their better
reafon and fuperior knowledge taught them it
was more to our intereft and welfare they fhould
only *voluntarily* proffer under *wife limitations,* we
vainly and madly attempted to exact one infinitely more hurtful and prejudicial for us to receive, than difficult, improper, or unjuft for them
to pay.   And the Commutation Act fhall teftify
to the lateft pofterity, and till time fhall be no
more, what the lofs of America has forrowfully
taught us,---that we were driven wild by prejudice and ignorance, and that it was unjuft, un-
wife, impolitic, and unprofitable, to pay fo high
a price for the *dried herbs even of China*; or, in
other words, to be mulct fo large a fine for mif-
taking

taking and deviating fo grofsly from the duties
of good financiers, prudent and difpaffionate
ftatefmen, as to raife the rate of teas, when our
interefts fhould have taught, and actually required
us, to lower it.---But this was the effect of unnatural prejudice, fupported by it's infeparable
companions, ignorance and obftinacy.

Turn our thoughts to the Eaftern World, and
we fhall find a parallel lofing game there alfo.
Here, as with America, we again find two
parties, which I may clearly diftinguifh by the
oppreffors and the *oppreffed*. On one fide, we
fee good and loyal fubjects, faithful fervants, and
unexceptionably good men, who, at an early period
of life having torn themfelves from their parents,
their kindred, and connexions, are devoting their
time, labours, healths, conftitutions, and lives,
in climates proverbial for their inclemency, to
the fervice of the Mother Country.---I fpeak of
the collective body---the community of Englifh
fubjects ferving in India, at large.---On the
other fide, prejudiced and ignorant politicians
converting themfelves into judges of their conduct, which they take on prefumption; unpro-
tecting mafters, or employers, who filently fuffer
their

their fervants to be cenfured and ftampt with
every frantic and opprobrious epithet, tho' wildly
foreign to truth; and obftinate, unfeeling fellow-
fubjects, whofe brains are filled with envy, hatred,
malice, and all uncharitablenefs; and whofe
brows exhibit avarice, extortion, difappointment,
difcontent, and ftrife, and their foul bantling prejudice, which they have nurtured and cherifhed like
a ferpent in their bofoms; and I boldly warn them
as the genuine dictate and belief of my foul, that
it deferves and will require their utmoft prudence
to avert it's pernicious and poifonous influence
from proving as calamitous and dreadful in it's
effects and confequences in the Eaftern, as it has
been in the Weftern dependencies of this deluded
kingdom.

In all cafes, it is our duty to hear reafon, and
to enquire and inform ourfelves before we venture
to decide; how much more, then, is it incumbent
on us to do fo, before we proceed to condemn:
and, in all cafes, there exifts fome certain and in-
difpenfable criterion, fome ftandard, by which the
human judgment ought to be regulated and governed. On the fubject we are to difcufs, let us
confider what that ftandard ought to be. It is

B   fuch

fuch as, I will venture to affert, the moft virulent prejudices, the 'moft partial, rancorous and envenomed mind will not dare openly to deny, however he may fecretly wifh to fupprefs.

Firft, we are infenfibly led to enquire, who the clafs of Britifh fubjects in India are, againft whom we are fo unnaturally prejudiced, and what their connexion or affinity with us ?

Secondly, the nature of their fervices; whether ufeful to us as a People, and ferviceable to the State; whether they are dutiful and loyal; whether they fhare with us the common labours and toils of life, it's duties and fervices in aid and maintenance of the Parent State, as their fubmiffion and allegiance require ?

Thirdly, whether they are entitled to our commendation, or our cenfure; our protection, and the juft and liberal reward of their country for their fervices; or its refentive condemnation and punifhment ?

Fourthly, of whom confift the party, what are their merits, or what the fervices they have rendered their country, who have thus affumed or arrogated to themfelves a right of jurifdiction

over

over their fellow-fubjects, kindred, and countrymen, ferving in India ?

This laft-mentioned object, it may be adverted,
is going beyond the boundary of a line purely de-
fenfive, in as much as a comparifon of conduct,
and principles of action, in favour of the gentlemen of India, here ftated to be the party *oppreffed*, may poffibly tend to throw much blame on the
people of England, and efpecially by proving
them but too juftly ftyled the *oppreffors*. The
defence of the former may fo unavoidably involve
the latter, that this may, in fome meafure, become an inevitable confequence; and will, of
courfe, be found highly warrantable; for, if the
people of England have affumed to themfelves a
right of jurifdiction over their fellow-fubjects in
India, which their relative fituation neither can
authorize, or which can at all be compatible with
their connexion, our countrymen in India certainly are not more unnatural in following only
fuch example; nor can they have lefs reafon and
juftification for peremptorily infifting on replacing
and maintaining themfelves in that juft degree of
equality which God and Nature gave them; and
of which, fo long as they demean themfelves as

good

good and loyal fubjects, God and Nature only can
have power to deprive them, however erroneoufly
or invidioufly their fellow-fubjects may attempt
it.

It affuredly is not my meaning, or at all to my
purpofe, ftudioufly to condemn my brethren of
England; fo far otherwife, I could wifh to find
them as fpotlefs in imputation, as they are generous in conduct; and as juft, as they are brave!
My fole purfuit is to refcue from the moft ignorant calumny, (for nothing lefs than ignorance
could give birth to fo grofs a fpecies of it,) and
to defend the abfent few, who, from the moft
laudable and loyal motives, are ferving their
country in India; alfo not to fuffer the hearts of
their fellow-fubjects to be detached, and their
affections alienated, while it is poffible that a fimple Appeal to felf-evident facts may conduce to
awaken them from unnatural delufion to the exercife of that fenfe and good underftanding with
which Nature has endowed them for the moft
benign purpofes, and prevent their fubmitting
themfelves to be impofed on by the ready-made
opinions of men of weak judgment and illiberal
minds, urged on by fpleen, envy, or jealoufy---

men

men mifled by every ill-founded and fhadowlefs
prejudice, with factious purpofes in view, de-
figning to blow up a conflagration that may for
ever fow the feeds of diffention, revive the ani-
mofity, and rekindle the fury of contending parties to fuch an unbridled degree, as may convulfe
the kingdom from one end to the other. I re-
peat, it is neither my meaning or purpofe to condemn: my only object and wifh is to defend a
very meritorious clafs of *ourfelves* from the unde-
ferved oppreffion of the reft; and, as from the
prefent public difcuffion of this fubject, and a late
popular decifion in a certain affembly, which fully
involves and carries with it an exculpation of the
foul imputations generally and indifcriminately
thrown on the community of Britifh fubjects in
India, we clearly perceive liberality of thinking
and acting on it, to be gradually diffufing itfelf
over the opinions of mankind, fttrong induce-
ments, and fome encouragement, influence me
to treat freely of their actual relative fituation,
firmly perfuaded, that if fentiments, founded on
the cleareft reafoning, and the moft unqueftion-
able facts, that fhall meet the underftanding of
every man capable of reflection, fhall fail of in-
fluencing

fluencing a converfion, and fhaking ill-founded
prejudice from the minds of my countrymen generally, they will, at leaft, obtain many advocates amongft men of liberal fentiments and enlightened minds, who, I am perfectly confident,
only require mifinformation to be removed from
their breafts, in order to correct and revoke opinions founded thereon; and who, it cannot one
moment be doubted, will feel themfelves fcanda-
lized in being thought to fuffer paffion or prejudice to influence their judgment one moment after the appearance of fact and truth. The judgment of a tribunal fo juftly difpofed, it muft be
the pride of every honeft man to obtain; poffeffing and regarding which as an ineftimable trea-
fure, he affumes a fecond dignity, and fcornfully
and contemptuoufly defpifes any fcattered feeds
of envy and jealoufy remaining elfewhere, as the
feeble refort of weak men and weaker minds, incapable of further mifchief. Supported by the
voice of the ferious few, he no longer regards the
clamour and noife of the thoughtlefs many.

Having thus candidly declared my object, and
the motives which have induced me to come
under the difcuffion and criticifm of the public
eye,

eye, where writers in general, however converſant with the world, however qualified to meet it, and whatever their merits, experience but little juſtice and leſs mercy, I do not think it improper to ſubjoin, with a view of obtaining a clearer title to an impartial and patient hearing, that I have not any other :---that I have not any party purpoſe to anſwer :---that I have not the moſt diſtant connexion with Miniſters, and that formidable phalanx ſuppoſed to be latently engaged in the protection of Eaſtern delinquents; and, moſt probably, never ſhall :---that if I wiſh one man to be Miniſter before another, my preference, inſignificant as it may be, is founded on and regulated by that ſimpleſt of all rules, " that I think him " the beſt qualified to render ſervice to his coun- " try" :---that, connected with very few of the gentlemen from India---with none who have ever had the power to do miſchief, or to bring the Engliſh name into diſrepute, it is a matter of indifference to me, what the public opinion of them in general may be, otherwiſe than as I revere the cauſe of truth, in which I am not aſhamed to be an advocate, however obnoxious the man ſuffering under it's ſuppreſſion.

To

To revert, then, to what ought to be the firſt
object of our enquiry---Who the claſs of Britiſh
ſubjects in India are, againſt whom we are ſo unnaturally prejudiced, and what their affinity or connexion with us?---

If it be poſſible, that an axiom of notoriety ever
came within the compaſs of the human underſtanding,---within the orthodox admiſſion of the
whole world, this is one of ſo long an eſtabliſhment
as almoſt to forbid the enquiry which I here propoſe
to make as an uſeleſs, unneceſſary, and idle trouble:
it moſt certainly ought to fall under that con-
ſtruction; but ſtill, experience has ſhewn on every
ſubject of diſcuſſion, generally, and on this in
particular, that the human underſtanding is naturally given to roam and to traverſe wide and even
beyond the limits of the point under conſideration,
abſolutely overlooking the vicinity within ocular
demonſtration, affording that ſureſt and moſt in-
dubitable evidence, which ought to have the firſt,
the earlieſt, and moſt effectual operation and influence upon our judgments. It has ſo manifeſtly
been the caſe in the inſtance before us, that I hold
it indiſpenſably neceſſary to recur to it, and endeavour to entice back my readers to the object
which

which they have unpremeditatedly paffed, and which it appears, has, confequently, wholly ef-caped their attention, or their recollection. They will forgive me, then, if, in the firft moment of time, I remind them---of what requires no argument to prove---that the Britifh fubjects, ferving their country in India, againft whom they fuffer fuch an unceafing torrent of invective, oppro-brium, and virulent condemnation, to run wildly loofe and madly frantic, *do not ftand in a lefs near degree of confanguinity* than their own children, whom they really are!---Gracious God! *our own children!*---Yes, your own children, whom you have nourifhed, fed, and reared with every pa-rental anxiety, but whom, not unlike the unna-tural object of Solomon's judgment, you have almoft given up to feverance, without once deign-ing to open your ears for information concerning the caufe, or reafoning on which fuch unnatural vi-rulence was founded --- for what mifconduct, or what crime, they have been thus difgracefully con-demned! Nature and time teach us affection and attachment; and inftinct mutually binds our yet inarticulate offspring to us, and us to our off-fpring. In what language, then, fhall we de-

C   fcribe---

ſcribe---in what colours ſhall we even reflect, or
ſuffer our imaginations lightly to touch, without
horror, on the baſe deſertion of thoſe duties which
we receive, as it were, by inſpiration ! Baſe deſertion ! I call it ; and hold it an infinitely more
unpardonable tranſgreſſion, in the ſight of that
awful Judge, "to whom all hearts ſhall be opened,
and from whom no ſecrets ſhall be hid," than any
ſpecies of criminality to be found delineated even
in the black catalogues of the crimes of a Jona-
than Wild, a Major Semple, Catharine Rudd,
or Warren Haſtings !

Not to dwell longer on a poſition ſo undeniable, I ſhall only add, that I appeal for the truth
of it to every individual who ſhall either read or
hear it, and will implicitly abide by the deciſion
of his own breaſt ; for it is next to a moral cer-
tainty, that it is ſcarce poſſible for any ſubject of
this kingdom to ſit in judgment amongſt the people, and not find, that he has either a ſon, a brother, a relation, or connexion, in the ſervice of
his country in the Eaſt. Even Mr. Haſtings
(who, from the documents before me, notwith-
ſtanding his long ſtudied endeavours to inculcate
a very different belief, as a convenient cover for
his

his own private purpofes, appears to have been no lefs the oppreffor of my countrymen ferving under him, than the natives of India fubject to his power) has defcribed, in his public advices, " many of them to be the fons of the firft families " in the kingdom of Great Britain." Mr. Haftings is by no means the greateft of all bigots to Truth; but in this felf-evident inftance, where no veil was to be found, he has certainly facrificed at her fhrine.

Having thus endeavoured to reftore you to the loft fight of your children,---your deareft connexions,---I fhall proceed to the fecond object of our enquiry, by no means lefs interefting, or inferior in it's confequences as affecting your paffions, or lefs important as it fhall concern your pride, viz. " The nature of the fervices of thefe your children in India,---whether ufeful to us as a people, or ferviceable to the State; whether they are dutiful and loyal; and whether they fhare in common with us the labours and toils of life, it's duties and fervices, in aid and maintenance of the Parent State, as their fubmiffion and allegiance require ?"

To minds liberally difpofed, and inclined to

C 2   reflection,

reflection, I fhould only trefpafs, by entering
largely into the wide expanfe which the above po-
fitions comprize; it would, virtually, be to detail
an hiftory of the Britifh governments in India for
a period of time little fhort of two complete cen-
turies; a work that would as far exceed my in-
tentions, or what is at all neceffary to my prefent
purpofe, as I am confident it would your expec-
tations : neither have I the prefumption to con-
ceive myfelf qualified, by the occafional diftribu-
tion of any allurements within the fcope of my
pen, and the humble fcale of its defcription, to
induce you to affume fuch an intolerable fund of
patience, as would be abfolutely neceffary to ac-
company me through it. Befides, while you can
turn to the fuperior, and, by this time, familiar
productions of Verelft and Orme, you cannot
poffibly defire me to call to your memories
more than their great leading features, if fo
much. I do not hefitate to conclude, you glad-
ly join iffue with me in this large retrenchment.

Our territorial acquifitions in India have long
been the admiration and the envy of the whole
European world; and, fince the feverance of
America, our quondam friends there have thrown
a lafci-

a lafcivious eye on them likewife. The peace was barely concluded, before the Thirteen Stripes were flying in the river Ganges, and a conteft begun with the Cuftom-Mafter at Calcutta, which was obliged to be *amicably fettled*, by the Americans lowering their ftandard, and hoifting (of all others !) the flag of France! It feems to be a queftion, on which time is wafted by the fages of the prefent day, philofophers, politicians, conftitutionalifts, and others *equally well informed*, whether the poffeffion of our Oriental dependencies be more a burthen or a benefit to this nation ? I find it has likewife crept into the fpeeches of fome of the national fenators, who have even advanced a ftep further, and wifhed the nation a perfect riddance of them. It is the loofe language of ftate quacks, iffued at random, which deferves no attention ;---the doctrine of men, infinitely more ufeful friends to our enemies than to us, who have no other means of obtruding themfelves into the knowledge of the Public. If our Eaftern fettlements be the admiration and envy of nearly the whole known World, which is a fact that will not be controverted, why ought they to be lefs valuable

to

to us ? Surely, if we did not before know the trea-
fures we poffeffed, the covetous thirft of our enemies after them fhould of itfelf awaken our fenfes
to their importance. Poffibly, they might be of
lefs comparative eftimation whilft we held good
fellowfhip with America; but, alas! the fituation of things is fo widely changed fince then, that
we muft now endeavour to retrieve in the Eaft
the dreadful loffes we have fuftained in the Weft.
An annual contribution of a million and an half,
and that greatly improveable, is no defpicable
aid to a nation like England groaning under tax-
ation, and burthened with a heavy debt, the annual intereft of which more than exhaufts the
whole of the national income; and, for this aid,
(or whatever the obftinate caviller will allow it to
be,) to whom are you indebted?---Not to the
King's Minifters---Not to the Eaft India Company, and their big-fwelling-pompous Directors,
for " *they toil not, neither do they fpin*";---but,
to *your abfent children*,---your own offspring,
who are ferving in the Eaft. It is to their merits
---to their induftry---to their activity---to their
good fenfe and prudence---to their difcreet ma-
nagement---to their labours and toils, and to the

heat

heat of their brows alone, that you are indebted for
the poffeffion of one of the moft, extenfive, the -
moft populous, and, probably, the richeft and
fineft countries in the world, and for every return of property, acquifition and wealth, of whatever denomination, that you derive from the Eaft.
---It is to their active zeal you owe the prefent
exalted ftate of the Eaft India Company, whofe
precedence in the commercial world is fo much
the object of your boaft :---it was their wife and .
enterprizing conduct which raifed them from a
confined trading company, without territory beyond the walls of a few fmall factories, barely on a
footing with the prefent humble ftate of thofe of the
French, Danes, Portuguefe, or Dutch, to their now
exalted condition of mercantile preeminence and
territorial dominion, with a princely income of
five millions fterling, a revenue which few poten-
tates in Europe can boaft.   It was their good and
fpirited conduct which refcued this *little body* from
the humiliating condition of being obliged to
refort to and depend on the too often perfidious
aid of our natural European enemies, their neigh-
bours, for a combined protection againft the op-
preffons of tyrant Muffulmen, and of enabling
them

them to prefcribe laws inftead of receiving them, in one inftance, and to grant that protection, in the other, for which themfelves were before the folicitors. It was thefe our brave and faithful brethren, in all comparatively but an handful, who overcame myriads before deemed invincible, and obtained thofe lafting monuments of your glory in Afia for their country's benefit:--- and, it was they who fubfequently raifed, difciplined, and attached armies to your fervice, whom they have repeatedly led to battle and to conqueft, thereby giving ftability and permanence to fuch vaft acquifitions :---In fhort, it is to them you are indebted for the poffeffion of *a fecond world !!!*---It is the literal exchange---the price which you receive for their blood fhed in their country's caufe, and their bones laid low in Eaftern foil, of which the extenfive European burial places at every fettlement in Afia will bear lafting teftimony*.---Yet thefe are the children whom

* To give my readers a competent idea of the ftate of mortality amongft Europeans in that country, where the individuals do not happily poffefs the expenfive means of counteracting the pernicious effects of it's climate, I need only

whom you fo haftily incline to abandon---to whom you envy the fmall participation of that immenfe wealth which their facrifices have procured you, confining your obfervation with an evil eye, to the *fortunate very few* who live to return and fhare with you their well-earned property in their native country!---Small as, God knows, this their portion of wealth is, when put in competition with the numbers of thofe who drop in the purfuit, and, amongft whom, were the whole to be divided, it would barely afford each half a loaf! Shall we, then, thus unthinkingly fuffer the imputation of envy to fmother our admired character for generofity of fentiment, and benevolence of heart, and withhold the effufions of gratitude where fo defervedly due?---Shall we, becaufe not immediately under our eye, overlook the abundant merits of this divifion of our fellow-fubjects, who, fent from their native country at an age of infancy, become refponfible to

only inftance the ftate of the Britifh foldiery, the eftablifhed number of whom ought to be *three thoufand*; to fupport which the Company fend an annual fupply of *from eighty to one hundred recruits by every fhip*, and yet are not able to effect it.—See Bengal Military Returns, feldom exceeding two thoufand.

a harda hard-judging world for their conduct, not only as men but as ftatefmen, at a period, when at home they are not emancipated from the fchool-mafter's difcipline ?---Shall we alfo overlook their merit at fuch an age of childhood in braving the rude ocean, and refifting the impetuous force of corrupt example during a fix month's voyage, where blafphemy unceafingly circulates in all it's moft horrid colours ?---Shall we likewife forget the fiery fhocks which their yet tender and unformed conftitutions experience in hoftile climes to the influence of which the ftrongeft frames muft bend ?---Shall we lofe fight of the dangers to which their young minds become expofed on their arrival by a communication with the moft vicious and luxurious fect of people inhabiting the world, who court them with every artful adulation, as fo many rifing funs through the influence of whofe rays they hope hereafter to benefit, and who endeavour to become panders to their paffions and their will, as a certain means of enflaving them to their future purpofes ?---

Can we, I fay, forget that with all thefe difadvantages of youth, inexperience, and temptation,

they

they prove themfelves honourable members of
fociety, fulfilling every character thereof, both
public and private, with virtue and integrity ?

Can we avow ourfelves fo uninformed, as to
deny to them thefe merits as a body, becaufe a
guilty few have, by their tyranny and oppreffion,
excited our juft indignation ? Can we really force
on ourfelves a belief, that there were none to be
found amongft them, whofe hearts were fanctu-
aries too holy for guefts fo vile ? Where is there
an equal body of men, with equal trufts, and
equal difadvantages, amongft whom fo few exceptionable characters are difcoverable ?---Muft
we, becaufe vice holds itfelf confpicuous in fome
daring characters, fuffer it's dark rays to overfhadow the brilliant virtues of the many ; and
thus allow integrity and abilities to be paffively
enveloped in the fteam of unrighteoufnefs ?

No, furely : our refentments at an end, we
fhall fenfibly feel the injuftice of fuch general
conclufions againft our fellow-fubjects in India ;
we fhall draw the juft line between merit and
mifconduct---between the innocent and the guilty ; and while we denounce juft punifhment on
conviction of the latter, we fhall not fail to diftri-

bute

bute ample reward to the former. But thefe merits cannot fo forcibly be exemplified, as by a fhort furvey of the nature of their fervices : to effect which, I fhall endeavour to paint their feveral and arduous avocations, in colours as juft as the informations and documents I have fo indefatigably aimed at collecting, will permit.

The Britifh fubjects, employed in India, are divifible into four defcriptions ; but, I fhall particularize Bengal, the feat of the Government General; as it is from the valuable manufciipts of a gentleman from thence I have derived very much affiftance.

The firft of thefe defcriptions confifts of the Officers of the Civil Government, and Officers having commiffions on the Military Eftablifhment, all, or the majority of whom, are gentlemen, and the fons of gentlemen, holding equality amongft the firft ranks of men, who will neither yield right of priority as fubjects, or for a moment acknowledge inferiority in loyalty and fidelity to their King and country. Their friends made an intereft for their election into the fervice of the Company, as a provifion for life, in what they were taught to believe and confider a purfuit

suit of honour and profit; and they have been
regularly admitted and enrolled, under ample
qualifications and credentials, and obtained fixed
rank and acquired rights on the public eftablifh-
ments. The number of civil fervants is about
two hundred and fifty, and the number of military officers about fifteen hundred: the duties
of the former, much the fame as the duties of
office in England, from the Firft Minifter of
State in the Cabinet, to the youngeft clerk at his
defk, in every department of the Britifh Government, and by no means lefs important; with a
variety of ftations, offices, and fervices, foreign
and domeftic, of much labour, difficulty, and
intricacy, unknown to the Civil Lift of England, all requiring ftudy, judgment, management, indefatigable application, and, what is
more than all, the difficult acquifition of Oriental
languages, and full infight into the characters,
religions, and prejudices of the natives. My
readers have an ample mode of detecting me, if
herein I err, by a reference to the annual Report
of the Eaft-India Company to the Honourable
Houfe of Commons, ftating the different offices
and employments of their fervants. But they
will

will readily admit, that the various duties of populous and extensive kingdoms like Bengal and Bahar, with all their branching foreign interests and connexions, which, involving all Hindostan and its vicinities, nearly communicate with the Continent of Europe itself, are not to be conducted with the ease and inactivity of a spinning-wheel, nor to be kept in regular routine by the approving nod of a powerful Minister, or the loud thunder of an able Oppositionist. As to military duties, you can ask no explanation. Let readers, who can judge of the general hardships of this service of honour, reflect but a moment on the additional toils of a brother soldier, labouring under the severities of a climate, where the thermometer in the sun is seldom less than 100, and, in situations where their duty calls them, many degrees higher; where a familiar acquaintance with the languages, manners, and religions of the men composing our armies, and where a study to invite and conciliate the natives bigotted to their own rules and prepossessions, and, subsequently, to gain and preserve the attachment of armies so composed, become a necessary part of the science. And, with respect to the general conduct of the army

of

of Bengal, I am warranted to aſſert, that it has
ever done them honour ; that they have exerciſed
their profeſſion with bravery, humanity, and mo-
deration ; and the inſtance of the Rohilla con-
queſt in 1774, exhibits the moſt noble inſtance
which hiſtory affords us of reſiſtance to the moſt
alluring temptations in the hour of plunder, when
they remained peaceable ſpectators of oppoſite
conduct in the troops of our ally. The ſecond
deſcription of Britiſh ſubjects comprizes the ve-
nerable Bench of Judicature, with all it's tribe of
officers, dependents, and followers, to the number of about one hundred, confiſting of Judges,
Barriſters, and a multitude of low, pettyfogging,
ignorant Attornies, who having *exchanged " brew-
ers aprons"* for *" Jacob's Law Dictionary,"* and
" Druggiſts weights and ſcales" for *" Every Man
his own Lawyer,"* have been admitted to prac-
tiſe, *ſecundum artem,* as quack doctors retail
their noſtrums, " no cure, no pay." This whole
corps, with a few exceptions of amiable and good
men, are virtually a flight of locuſts, " ſeeking
whom to devour," and will prove an everlaſting
ſtain on the wiſdom of the Legiſlature, whoſe act
is their licence, ſo long as one ſtone of this in-
ſtitution

ftitution fhall remain on another. And, what is
their object ?——Precifely, " to *fow diffention*
" *amongft their fellow-citizens, and to get money* !"
Lawyers are certainly the laft clafs of profeffional
beings who fhould be admitted into a country
where the form of Government is yet immature.
They profefs mifchief ;—they make mifchief, and
they unmake mifchief; they have mifchief in
their mouths, and they have mifchief at their
fingers ends !—And yet, they are called the
" Independent Corps !" Their late leader in
Calcutta certainly placed little apparent value on
his claim to that diftinction, as he literally " part-
" ed with his birth-right for a mefs of pottage ;"
but the Lawyers, not chufing to ape their bright
luminary in this his new orb,ftill maintained their's,
and when, during the late war, the Britifh fubjects
in Bengal were required to form themfelves into
a militia, the Lawyers pleaded their independence
of the Company's government, and the affiftance
of a fearch warrant muft have been required to
have found any one of them on the parade on
field days. This certainly was one fpecies of
independence, and is a tolerable good fpecimen of
the acutenefs of their talents for perverfion.—

Their

Their continuance abroad is not only very unne-ceffary, but very pernicious, as the execution of Nuncomar, on an *ex poft faƈto* law, and the hea-vy loffes the Company have fuftained by their of-ficious interference, have evinced. And, having thus defcribed the fecond clafs of our country-men in India, as I fhall have no occafion to re-vert to them, or their purfuits, I fhall difmifs them with a moft ferious recommendation to the nation at large, to infift on their evacuating Ben-gal without delay---in fome fuch mode as Mr. Haftings recalled the reprefentative of the Britifh nation from the Court of Lucknow *.

The third clafs confifts of a few Clergymen, upwards of an hundred Surgeons and Apothe-caries in the civil and military employ of the

    " Mr. Richard Johnfon.
  " Sir,
  " You are hereby peremptorily ordered and commanded,
" within forty-eight hours of the receipt of this letter, to
" quit Lucknow, and repair without delay to the Prefidency
" of Fort William.— We have further to acquaint you, that
" the Commanding Officer at Cawnpore [a military ftation]
" has been direƈted to enforce thefe orders, in cafe of dif-
" obedience on your part."—See India Papers, vol. ii,
p. 25.

E   Company,

Company, the exercife of whofe functions there are the fame as in every other part of the world ; and about as many free merchants, a refpectable body of gentlemen, who, although not covenanted fervants of the Company, have their fanction to refide, and engage themfelves in private commerce, and many of whom have rendered very effential fervices to the nation ; but particularly a gentleman, who lately gave evidence in an honourable Affembly on the fubject of opium, and whofe fervices are on their records. See India Papers, Vol. VI. p. 22.

The fourth and laft clafs includes a moft ufeful body of pilots, feamen, handicrafts, and mechanicks, whom fervice, neceffity, or chance, have introduced, and who are there by fufferance, and, probably, without any exprefs licence from the Company ; and a corps of well-difciplined troops, to the number of about two thoufand, whofe duty, as in other armies, fimply confifts in obedience.

Let us now proceed to examine, how the duties of the government are fulfilled.

The whole world bear teftimony of the great and enviable advantages accruing from our poffef-

fions in India,---advantages not derived from
chance or magical influence, which muft follow,
if our brethren in India poffefs no merit, but
entirely from the prudent management and able
conduct of thefe our brethren, to which only we
are beholden for every importation of wealth or
property from thence.---In this kingdom we
juftly hold up as a prodigy a fingle inftance of
youth, becaufe, with the advantages of a finifhed
education, and the affiftance of wife and experienced counfellors, deemed capable of guiding
the helm of a ftate; and great, it muft be ac-
knowledged, is his merit.---But, fhall we at the
fame time deny what is due to our ftill younger
brethren in the Eaft, whofe abilities in the fame
various branches are equally called into action,
executed with equal judgment, integrity, and fuc-
cefs, although removed from their ftudies at a
period of life, when the moft brilliant part of their
education would only have commenced, and
whofe further improvement can alone be the
effect of their own fole merit.---Let us not fuppofe the government of India to be a mere
fyftem of trade and plantation. The civil government is divided into three diftinct branches,

comprifing

comprifing the political, the revenue, and the commercial departments; into each of which the civil fervants of the Company are ftationed as their talents and capacities render eligible, and they gradually rife in their refpective lines,--- with few exceptions, circumftances fometimes occurring to occafion a removal from the one branch to the other : and this fhould account in England to fuch as appear furprized at finding gentlemen return from India not equally converfant in each of thefe diftinct and extenfive departments; add to which the orders of the Company prohibiting* their fervants from a free accefs to the

* *Extract of a General Letter from the Honourable the Court of Directors, to the Honourable the Governor General and Council, dated 21ft Sept.* 1785.

Paragraph 50. We have long regretted an abufe which is now become fo prevalent, and has gone to fuch an extent, that we muft be peremptory in taking the moft effectual meafures to put an end to it. We allude to the practice of our fervants having accefs to and tranfmitting home to their private correfpondents, fuch part of our Records as they think proper. Our orders, therefore, are, that no perfon but the Members of the different Boards fhall have accefs to their Records, except the Secretaries of fuch Boards, and thofe entrufted by them; and that no private copies fhall be given thereof, except to the Prefident of each Board, if he fhall

the records of any other department than that
to which they immediately belong, although they

fhall defire it. To thefe perfons fo entrufted we fhall look
for refponfibility; and if copies of any of our papers, cor-
refpondence, or Records, fhall be difcovered in the poffeffion of any perfons not warranted by the Government either
at home or abroad, we fhall certainly take the moft effectual
meafures in our power to difcover by whofe means the communication has been made, and will difmifs from our fervice any perfon who fhall be found guilty of difobeying
thefe our orders.

51. Another practice of a fimilar nature likewife calls for
our animadverfion. Many of our fervants poffeffing our
moft confidential fituations are accuftomed to indulge themfelves, without referve, in correfponding, by their private
letters, upon the public affairs of the Company. This is
attended with many inconveniencies, is directly contrary to
our repeated orders, and we defire you will take the moft
effectual means to prevent it; and if any of our fervants
prefume to continue in a practice fo contrary to our wifhes
and orders, we fhall certainly mark our difapprobation by
the fevereft tokens of our difpleafure.

52. It is incumbent upon us further to inform you, that
a practice has fometimes prevailed of late, of our fervants
abroad fending home public letters to the care of perfons
refident in this country, to be delivered by them or not, as
in their difcretion they fhall think proper: we prohibit any
fuch practice in future; and direct that all letters to us from
our fervants abroad, be addreffed directly to the Court of
Directors, and fent by the ufual conveyance; no other will
be received by us.

profeffedly

profeffedly expect their fervants to be qualified
for all departments.---In the political line the
number can be but few; yet among thefe we find
finifhed ambaffadors, prudent negociators, and
able ftatefmen.---The revenue branch is more
diffufe, and it's duties more complicated and arduous, yet executed with that fuperior degree of
judgment, punctuality, and ability, which only
requires to be known to excite both our admiration and aftonifhment.---The bufinefs of this department is intricate, laborious, and manifold,
inafmuch as it comprizes all the various duties of
a minifter;---of civil and criminal magiftracy;---
of inveftigator of the refources of provinces;
---of affeffor and receiver of revenue;---of
comptroller of taxes, duties, and cuftoms;---and
of treafurer, &c. &c. with all the moft difficult
management of finance; add to which a competent knowledge of the languages, manners,
fuperftitions, cuftoms, and corrupt practices of
the various fects of people refiding within their
extenfive jurifdictions, whofe undermining intrigues, inceffantly at work, require the moft active and vigilant ability, and which it is not poffible too warily to counteract.---Here we find

youths

youths governing populous and extenfive provinces, many of them nearly as large as Great
Britain itfelf---youths prefiding in crowded courts
of juftice, hearing caufes and appeals from thou-
fands in their refpective languages, and deciding
with juftice, integrity, and univerfal fatisfaction.---
How few of thefe provincial decifions have ever
been arraigned of error or injury, and how ftill
fewer it has ever been found proper to reverfe,
even Sir Elijah Impey, who prefided over the
Court of Appeals at the Prefidency of Fort William, and whofe bitter prejudices againft the
fervants of the Company are on record, cannot
fcruple to bear teftimony.

Nor is the commercial department, though
ftanding in order the laft, of the leaft importance to
this country, as it is to the judgment and good
conduct exercifed in this line, that this kingdom,
and, virtually, every part of the globe where the
products of the Eaft are in eftimation, are indebted
for the great improvement of their manufactures,
and for thofe well-chofen inveftments fent home
by the fervants of the Company, which annually
allure the whole European world to our ports and
markets. The magnitude and importance of
thefe

thefe advantages will not be difputed ; but, great
as they are, I find by enquiry, that, had the re-
commendations of the fervants abroad been duly
attended to and fupported by Directors and Minifters at home,thofe advantages would have been
greatly multiplied.---For the want of a grateful
communication of property between that country
and this kingdom, individuals have been help-
lefsly driven into the arms of other nations for the
remittance of their fortunes, and thereby have
enabled foreigners to carry on a trade, in a country, the commerce of which we profefs to claim the
exclufive* privilege of,nearly co-extenfive with our
own, almoft wholly on credit :---whereas, had the
Company opened their treafury, as they *ought to
have done*, for remittances at a liberal rate of exchange, even *decently* within the terms of foreign bills †, and *augmented their inveftments* accordingly,

___

* This " exclufive privilege", *to our difgrace be it fpoken,*
affects only the fubjects of Great Britain and Ireland, thofe
of all other nations having a free intercourfe with all the
Eaftern fettlements, whether thofe of England, or otherwife.

† Foreign bonds on refpondentia under a fpecific mort-
gage of the fhip and cargo, at an exchange of 2s. 3d. the
current rupee, and ten per cent. premium, while you may
enfure for fix, payable in London nine months after the arrival

cordingly, they would have *multiplied the national
advantages :*---they would have *multiplied their
own.* Such meafures would *have encreafed the
cuftoms ;*---would have *encreafed the national
ftrength* by *encreafing their fhipping,* which, fitted
out armé en flute, might have been converted into
fhips of war as occafion fhould require :---would
have eftablifhed a certain and infallible nurfery for
feamen, that moft important objeft to England,

rival of the fhip at her deftined port.—For the terms offered
by the Englifh Company, read their own words,—when
they laft authorized bills to be drawn—viz. in Sept. 1785.—
   " All thefe bills, both for the bonded and the other debts,
are to be drawn at an exchange of one fhilling and eight
pence the Bengal current rupee, and at a proportionable
rate of exchange for the pagoda and Bombay rupee, to be
fettled by our Governor General and Council. They are
to be made payable 548 days after date, with an option to
the Company to poftpone the full payment thereof, on paying intereft upon them half yearly, at the rate of 5 per cent.
per annum, from the date of their becoming due, and alfo
on paying inftalments of not lefs than 10 per cent. on the
principal in every year, after the 1ft March 1790, unlefs it
fhall fuit our convenience to difcharge them by earlier or
larger payments ; and for the purpofe of rendering thofe
bills more convenient to the holders, they are to be iffued
to each creditor in bills of five hundred pounds each, and
one bill for the fraftional part, if any fuch fhall be owing to
him."

F   now

now fo much wanted :---would have given em-
ployment to large bodies of people; prevented
competition with the foreign world, and, by re-
ducing them to the neceffity of importing bullion
for the fupport of their remaining trade, as for-
merly, they would have aided our fettlements by
the introduction of fpecie, inftead of the difadvantages of it's drain, from the effects of which
they have for fome time paft been drooping.---
This is a fubject of fo much ferious moment to
this nation, that it is entitled to claim the particular attention of it's Minifters, and the whole
fhipping interefts; nor can I omit this opportu-
nity of *teftifying to the People of England at large*,
that if, from the affumption of the Bengal Government by Lord Clive in 1767 to the prefent
time, 1787, there be any one point of duty in
which their brethren ferving abroad have been
more uniform than another, it has been the recommendation of this fubject to the confideration
and adoption of their employers.

From the foregoing fhort premifes, I truft,
the generous reader will readily feel and acknowledge with me, that the fervices of thefe
our abfent brethren are highly meritorious and
" ufeful

" ufeful to the State; that they are dutiful and
" loyal, and *more* than fhare in common with us
" the labours and toils of life, it's duties and
" callings, in aid and maintenance of the Parent
" State:"---and, from hence will alfo conclude,
in the terms of the third queftion of our invefti-
gation, " That they are juftly entitled to our
" moft grateful commendation, and not our cen-
" fure---to our warm protection, and the juft and
" liberal reward of their country, for their fer-
" vices, and not to it's refentive condemnation
" or punifhment."

It now only remains to confider the fituation
and merits of thofe moft eager to become the general and illiberal cenfurers of fo large and refpectable a part of ourfelves, who, without being
at the trouble of reflection or enquiry, have, from
the alledged mifconduct of a few, arrogated to
themfelves the right of paffing fentence on the
whole.

Among thefe I can only difcover perfons poffeffing the *negative merit* of inheriting rank or
independence from the virtue or toils of their
anceftors; whofe *moft fatiguing expedition* has been
a " fummer trip to the Continent, in fearch of an

" Opera

" Opera dancer," and whofe *moſt glorious exploit*
has confifted in a " fuccefsful elopement, where
" no refcue was attempted ;" or others, moving
in the more humble fphere of aping their betters
in the repetition of common-place opinions, as
the moſt promiſing mode of fecuring their future
favour. Surely, thefe ought not to prove leaders
of fufficient weight to bias the judgment of the
people of England, whofe juſtice, on reflection,
will ever teach them to queſtion their own right
of paſſing fentence, as well as the grounds on
which they proceed ; and until they forfeit the
character of Britons, they will be as cautious in
aſſuming a competency of judgment improperly,
as tenacious in it's maintenance when admitted.
Yet, for want of fuch reflection, I am forry to
fay, the jurifdiction has not only been aſſumed,
but they have actually proceeded to judgment---
haſtily, I will admit; but neverthelefs carrying
with it all the poignancy of condemnation and
confequent prejudice, with ſtrong indications of
which the prefs at prefent teems ; and the " de-
" linquency and peculations of our fervants
" abroad," come as pat from the mouths of
every porter at the India Houfe, as " the laſt
" dying,

" dying fpeech and confeffion of the malefactors
" executed at Tyburn," from that of the but-
cher's parrot of St. Martin's Court; and though
with as little intellectual connexion, yet as eager-
ly liftened to by the wondering and credulous
multitude.

The terms " delinquents" and " peculators,"
appear to be received as fynonymous defcriptions
of gentlemen ferving abroad; yet it is by no
means free from apprehenfion, that too ftrict an
enquiry would prove them infinitely more appli-
cable to thofe of correfponding ftations in England. But, with what eye would the injuftice of
the gentlemen from India be regarded, were they
therefore to pronounce indifcriminate cenfure ?---
However, admitting mifconduct among our brethren of the Eaft, (for what but imperfection is
the lot of humanity !) it clearly can only be confined to a few. Mifconduct neceffarily implies a
pre-exifting power to incur it; common fenfe
teaches, that few there are in any Government,
who can poffefs that power; and that it can only
be among thofe few that we can look for refponfibility: therefore, the accufer, be he who he
may, previous to condemnation, fhould difpaf-

fionately and deliberately queftion himfelf as to
the power of the party arraigned, and regulate
his opinions accordingly. The Britifh inhabitants of the Eaft are no more *all rulers indivi-*
dually, than the whole people of England : it
would be prepofterous to fuppofe it ; but it would
not be more prepofterous to condemn the whole
people of England on that ground of conftructive
abufe and oppreffion, than it is to involve, under
indifcriminate condemnation, the whole body of
Britifh fubjects in Afia. Much pains have been
taken to load with opprobrium a fervice, which,
in itfelf, is indifputably honourable ; but wherein
can the difference of fervice between England
and Afia confift, the purfuit being fo much the
fame, as to entitle the former to imply purity,
while the latter fhall only infer contamination ?
The moft rigid analyfis will prove to an axiom,
how ridiculous the doctrine ;---it will evince, to
mathematical demonftration, that the object of
both fervices is alike a mixture of honour and
profit ; that wealth is not lefs our purfuit at home
than abroad. But here, I apprehend, the comparifon between our brethren of India and ourfelves, will not prove favourable to us, if we re-

vert

vert to the difficult, dear bought, and far fought rewards of the one, and to the fatisfactory eafe of the obtaining it at home in the bofom of their native country, amidft their families and friends, and without the facrifice of health, or any one enjoyment that can attend life, by the other :---- thefe laft, moreover, poffefs not the plea of having a competency to feek, which, as I have before faid, they already have the negative merit of deriving from their anceftors, but are actuated by the inordinate thirft of accumulation; whereas, the former go profeffedly in fearch of a well-earned competency, which, when acquired, they return to fhare hofpitably amongft their countrymen. And fhall we, my friends, think even the meaneft of our fellow-fubjects in this kingdom entitled to enjoy unmolefted the fruits of his induftry, and deny the fame privilege to thofe who have paid fo dearly for the acquifition of independence, in the accomplifhment of our aggrandizement abroad? Or, can we fuppofe, that the official advantages in that country, any more than in this, are confined to nominal, inadequate falaries! We need only have recourfe to the Kalendar to fatisfy ourfelves on what an unreafonable

ground

ground fuch an expectation would here be form-
ed ; and wherefore affect furprize at the exiftence
of emolument in India, beyond the falaries an-
nexed, which, in that country, are not even
equal to the moft rigid frugality ;---but, were
they even a *decent* maintenance, could we reafonably expect gentlemen to quit their native country, their families, and friends, in purfuit of a
mere temporary fubfiftence, and thereby fubfcribe
to banifhment, like felons tranfported for life,
without hope of return ! If the fervice of the
Eaft be a fervice of emolument, as it undoubt-
edly is, and certainly ought to be, the fervice
of England is not lefs fo ; and I venture to pronounce, without the fear of contradiction, that
they are alike avowed, and fo equally well un-
derftood, as alike to have obtained fanction from
the neceffity of toleration. But, we need not
inftance either England or India; all fervices
whatever have their foundation in emolument,
which forms the cement of affociation, and
creates the only title we can make to the affiftance
of our fellow-creatures.

It may here be alledged, that India Delinquency ftands actually before the nation in moft glaring

ing colours. But, let us for a moment examine the situation of parties so arraigned, and we shall find, that they are wholly confined to such individuals, as in a former part of their lives, having returned with moderate fortunes and reasonable views, were corrupted by the intrigues and evil example of those at home, to answer different views, and taught so well to feel the necessity of abundant riches in this extortionate country, as to make them desperate in their resolves on future acquisitions at any price. I am perfectly warranted to use this last, though harsh expression; for, who can deny, that the gentlemen from India, immediately on their landing in England, become objects of general prey to plunderers of all denominations? This, without the sting of the present fashionable vices, so well understood within the precincts of St. James', has not a little contributed to drive many of them back again, while others, failing in this expedient, have actually sunk under the weight of it's oppression.

But, it may be said, the general condemnation before alluded to has even originated from the authority of the head of their own community.

G   (See

(See Mr. Hafting's Letters from Bengal, 5th
May 1781, and from Lucknow, 30th April
1784, &c.)

How far the fentiments contained in thofe letters were dictated by truth, or what oppofite im-
preffions they were calculated to effect, the People of England can by this time form a competent judgment. I am happy to fee that my countrymen, thus injured, have found protection in
the lights thrown thereon by Mr. Burke's bright
and able exertions; for, in a Government confti-
tuted like that of Bengal, where our fuperiority
is more ideal than real, the *governing* being fo
out of all proportion to the *governed*, the degra-
dation or depreffion of the Englifh name and
character is by no means the leaft exceptionable
part of a Governor's conduct. The before-
mentioned Letters would lead us to believe, that
all in India were corrupt, *except the author*; but,
unlefs the fyftem of ethics be reverfed, it is mo-
rally *impoffible* for the *body to be fo univerfally
difeafed, and the head remain unpolluted.* Who-
ever fhall be at the pains of perufing the Letters
in queftion, will readily admit the juft fentiments
contained in the late celebrated oration of an
honorable

honorable Member of the Houſe of Commons,
that " ſuch imputations on the Engliſh name
" were moſt readily and joyfully countenanced
" as a ſcreen and ſhelter for his own (the au-
" thor's) abandoned profligacy."---For my own
part, I ſhall only further obſerve, that *thoſe
productions are the Author's own libels on his
own adminiſtration.*

It may be obſerved, that the object of this
condemnation is not the acquiſition of wealth,
but the practices of cruelty whereby it is obtained. This is a worn-out charge, which never
could be verified. The Britiſh inhabitants of
India have on more occaſions than one loudly
applied to their country, (ſee Comments on their
Petition to Parliament, in the year 1779,) " to
" call forth from amongſt them any individuals
" whoſe conduct was exceptionable, to conviction
" and puniſhment," and even offered their ſer-
vices " to aſſiſt in the proſecution ;"---but, from
that hour to this, no caſe of guilt has ever been
preſumed, except in the inſtances of a certain
Baronet, and a late Governor General : the firſt
is recent within the mind of every man, as it regularly underwent a Parliamentary enquiry : the

ſecond

fecond is now before them; and, if he be that
honeft man he announces himfelf, like an honeft
man he will defire to go to his trial, and, like an
honeft man, be acquitted.

But, my good friends, admitting for a moment what is *moſt diametrically oppoſite to the
truth,* that cruelties have been practiſed. If a
zealous abhorrence of fuch acts be your motives,
you have a very extenſive field before you, for
the exercife of your clemency, in the long fanc-
tioned practices of the Weſt Indies, where flavery
and cruelty are reduced to a fyſtem, and human
nature is your traffic *. While you publicly
countenance fuch practices as thefe, to what fhort
of envy can be attributed your ftrictures on your
brethren in the Eaſt ? It will be difficult to per-
fuade future ages, that your condemnation of
alledged conduct in one part of the world is the

---

* I have been well affured, that, in the Weſt Indies,
flavery is reduced to fo complete a fyſtem, that planters
there make regular calculations by which they are governed
in the treatment of their flaves, and from which they find it
more beneficial to work their flaves to death in the fhort
fpace of three years, than to allow them the courfe of nature's fpan in the performance of ordinary duty.

effect

effect of humanity, while you *publicly* enjoy the benefits arifing from the *open fale* of your fellow-creatures in another ! !

Having thus offered a vindication of the conduct of my countrymen againft private prejudice and public reprefentation, let us advert a little to fome public acts of this nation, whereby they have juft reafon to confider themfelves injured.

In 1773, we paffed an act under the plea of correcting prevalent abufes in the adminiftration of the Company's affairs both at home and abroad, which, by depriving them of their natural right of trial by jury, the great palladium of the freedom of England, became an arbitrary and unjuft oppreffion ; and this was farther aggravated by the inftitution of a Court of Judicature, vefting in the Judges, or at leaft leaving them the power to affume an undefined jurifdiction, accompanied by a fpecies of difcretion in the difpenfation of juftice, unknown to the fyftem of jurifprudence and the practice of the Courts in Great Britain, by which thefe Judges virtually became Legiflators alfo. Meafures of fuch tendency require no comment to an Englifh reader. But, injurious as they were to the birth-

rights

rights of Englishmen, let us examine with what temper they were received in India. The operation of this institution commenced in Bengal in the year 1774. It is not to be supposed our brethren there could be insensible to so gross a grievance, or that their minds could be otherwise than filled with alarm, at thus becoming the objects of measures so unconstitutional, and far more calculated to multiply than to remedy the evils which they were professedly to remove.--- They neverthelefs received the act with the deference due to the authority from whence it issued, and unmurmuringly submitted to it's practice and effects, for a period of near five years, in order to give it a full and uninterrupted trial; and, then only, on bitter experience of it's baneful confequences, came forward in a modest and respectful appeal to their country, signed by six hundred and forty-eight as good and loyal fubjects as any in his Majesty's dominions, for that redrefs to which they were so well entitled.--- But, I am forry to cast so great a flur on the honor and justice of my country, as to observe these grievances, crying as they are, still unredressed: nay, we have, on the contrary, even

added

added infult to injury, by the fubfequent act of
1784, not only by divefting them of other rights
and privileges derived from their fituation and
length of fervices, but, to the difgraceful encouragement of bafe informers, who, in that country
in particular, are ever ready to facrifice their
mafters, or protectors, to fordid purpofes. I
fhall not enlarge on that claufe of the act which
was a monument of fo much glaring difgrace to
our nation, that it's framers found it wife to
repeal it. I muft, however, obferve, that the
infult it offered was complete in the enacting it,
as it fully and ftrongly expreffed the ill-founded
angry bias which raged in the minds of their
countrymen againft them. The claufe in allufion
cannot fail to be in the recollection of my reader;
but, to bring to his mind the full influence of it's
injurious tendency, let him reflect with what temper fuch a claufe would be received among the
people of England, and more particularly among
the Members of that very Houfe, who framed
and paffed the act for others.

Still unredreffed, the grievances of our fellow-
fubjects in India now form the fubftance of a fecond petition to their country, which has, at
length,

length, found its way to the table of the Houfe of Commons; but, under fo many difficulties and difcouragements, as to damp the profpect of the redrefs reafonably looked for; at leaft, fhould any weight be given to the extraordinary opinion of an honorable minifterial Member on the motion for it's introduction, who, if he did not confider the petitioners as the *inanimate property* of the Eaft-India Company, clearly reduced them to the ftate of live ftock; for, " how," fays he, " can we receive a petition from thofe " who are only the fervants of the Company, " when the Company themfelves [or, in other " words, *thefe gentlemen's owners*] have not peti- "tioned!" As the difcuffion of India bufinefs, from the confpicuous and exalted ftation which this honorable Member fills, muft completely abforb his thoughts at prefent; and as it is by no means unufual with him to trample on all *diftinctions of locality*, fo, on this occafion, he muft certainly have tranfported his mind's eye from Calcutta, the refidence of *gentlemen not in any refpect his inferiors*, to the wretched fcene of Englifh avarice and defpotifm in Rohilcund, where *our humane ally* the tyrant Sujah Dowlah, " having [it is " faid]

" faid] converted the Rohillahs into fubjects, the
" next thing he does is to deny them the rights
" of human creatures, and palpably confider them
" as inanimate property, which the owner may
" difpofe of as he thinks fit."---Good Heavens!
what a doctrine! I congratulate my country,
however, that it did not proceed from the *mouth
of an Englishman*; and that the rectitude of a
British Houfe of Commons fcouted fuch fentiments with the fcorn they deferve. We ought
not, however, to be affected with furprize at the
fpeech in queftion, when we reflect, that the petition againft which it argued, was produced by
the oppreffive act which this very Member is fup-
pofed to have had fo ample a fhare in framing,
and of which the moft offenfive claufe (faid to
have been his favourite bantling) but too plainly
characterizes it's author, and his talents for defpotifm.

We fhall not relinquifh the hope of feeing the
natural juftice of Parliament exerted in a due
attention to the reafonable prayer of the petition
of thefe our fellow-fubjects. An Englifh Houfe
of Commons has ever hitherto gloried in oppofing
unconftitutional meafures---and they would de-

H   fert

fert their duty if they did not: fuch inftances, therefore, of encroachment, as now aggrieve our fellow-fubjects in India, can only be attributed to minifterial faction; and, confequently, it is to be prefumed, cannot be of much longer duration. Juftice will ever prove a fufficient fpur to Englifhmen, without having recourfe to the additional motive of caution againft driving the oppreffed to fuch defperate acts as the ftrength of a powerful army, confifting of fifteen hundred experienced officers, and fixty thoufand brave and well-difciplined troops, attached to them from affection and fervice, in poffeffion of a rich and extenfive country, yielding a moft princely revenue, and fraught with every valuable refource, might enable them to effect. But, fhould Minifters perfift in turning a deaf ear to the juft claims of the petitioners, becaufe they poffefs the power fo to do, and determine to with-hold rights, to the poffeffion and free exercife of which, the loyalty, fidelity, and great atchievements of our brethren in India, in their country's caufe, would of themfelves be deemed an ample title under more reafonable men, I fhall moft earneftly recommend it to fuch rulers,

to

to turn their reflections to the fatal and yet bleed-
ing effects experienced from fuch unfeeling and
injudicious conduct towards our late brethren in
America; whofe perfecution, as I before faid,
" originated in prejudice, was conducted in ig-
" norance, and has concluded in compulfive fe-
" verance." Our fellow-fubjects in the Eaft have
fhewn, that they can bear diftrefs like men, and
feel like men; and while we fhall continue to
poffefs our valuable acquifitions in that country,
which we at prefent hold on a tenure of perpe-
tuity as the tribute of their eminent fervices, and
which nothing can fhake, while we continue to
poffefs their affections and attachment unfhaken,
we certainly cannot require to be reminded, that
they can alfo *act like men*. Let us, then, beware
how we drive them to extremities; nor, when
they apply to us for bread, prefent them a ftone.
Our errors towards them are hitherto retriev-
able with honor;---but, leaving the protection
of their petition to the more able and interefted
advocates acting under their immediate delega-
tion, I fhall not further trefpafs on the patience
of my readers. The object of this Appeal is of
a different nature; and I dare truft, the candid

H 2

and

and generous minds of my countrymen, ever
open to conviction, particularly in the caufe of
TRUTH, will have fuffered my juft, though un-
adorned arguments, to remove the veil of prejudice from their underftandings, nor longer allow " the dark rays of vice, confpicuous in a
" few daring characters, to overfhadow the bril-
" liant virtues of the Many, and thus fuffer in-
" tegrity and abilities to be paffively enveloped
" in the fteam of unrighteoufnefs :"---that they
will not confound particular error with general
merit and loyal fervice; nor forget, that their
*fellow-fubjects in India are a part of themfelves,
and have never yet been deficient in their country's
caufe.*

An apology to the Public for an intrufion on
their time, generally precedes the fubject; and,
although I feel the neceffity of it greater in my
inftance than in any other, I ftill flatter myfelf it
will not be lefs favorably received, as a conclu-
fion, than if I had, in the ufual way, made it in
a formal exordium. I may fafely place great
reliance on the difintereftednefs of my motive;
but more powerfully reft on the neceffity which
humanity laid me under, of taking up a caufe,
which,

which, in the opinion of unprejudiced people, has been *moſt ſhamefully abandoned by gentlemen, whoſe former ſtations in India, and preſent ſituations in an Honorable Aſſembly, render it their more immediate province, if not their duty,* which can no otherwiſe be accounted for, than as the effect of the miſtaken principle, of ſuppoſing it neceſſary to ſacrifice the whole community of their India brethren to the deſperate cauſe of an individual.---And this abandonment is the more ſhameful, as the expectation of the nation is naturally directed to them in particular, for a juſtification of their former ſociety; and that their ſilence, however indefenſible, may be conſtrued into condemnation: they ſhould, however, reflect, that this condemnation muſt in a more material degree affect themſelves, not only from their affinity of power and conſequent reſponſibility, with the individual in queſtion, but from the dread of inveſtigation, which this their ſilence might imply.---Should this hint tend to awaken them from their unpardonable lethargy, it will prove a great additional reward for any pains I may have been at in collecting materials for the juſtification of my fellow-countrymen abroad, which, in my

opinion,

opinion, requires nothing more than a fimple ftate of facts amply and firmly to eftablifh.---
I have done my duty, as a good citizen, in contributing my mite towards it ; and thereon found a claim to call on thefe gentlemen, either to follow my example, or to avow the motives of their defertion of what muft be no lefs their own, than the caufe of our abfent countrymen.

F I N I S.

.

9 7 8 3 3 3 7 0 5 9 1 6 3